Advanced Praise
Brilliant Stars Are Born"

"Reading David Sterken's Out of Chaos... had such a profound impact on me. It touched both my soul and my spirit in wonderfully unexpected ways. Though there is some prose here in the form of actual journal entries, Sterken's book is mostly comprised of brutally honest and poignantly heartfelt poetry. Centered around the themes of addiction, self-worth, forgiveness and, ultimately, redemption, these are some of the most spiritually-attuned, yet readily accessible poems I've read in recent years. Sterken's powerful and candid collection seemed to support and affirm my own spiritual path, and I look forward to revisiting these beautiful poems again and again."

Salvatore Sapienza, author of *Gay is a Gift*

First Edition 2010

All Rights Reserved Copyright 2010
By Brilliant Star Press

Out Of Chaos Brilliant Stars Are Born

All rights reserved. No part of this book may be reproduced or transmitted in any form or by any means, graphic, electronic or mechanical, including photocopying, recording, taping, or by any information storage or retrieval system, without the permission in writing from the publisher, except where permitted by law.

www.brilliantstarpress.com

Printed in the United States of America

Out Of Chaos Brilliant Stars Are Born/David J. Sterken

ISBN: 978-1449949792

Out Of Chaos
Brilliant Stars Are Born

David J. Sterken

Dedication

This book is dedicated to my mother, Dorothy Belle Sterken, who spent hours with me as a young writer helping me develop my skills. Much to my chagrin she often made me rewrite entire papers encouraging me to use words to make my stories come alive. I owe her my thanks for recognizing my gift and fostering it through creative expression.

Secondly, I want to thank my angels – those of you who have supported me on my journey. At times you did so without knowing the depth of what was going on, but you loved me nonetheless. I cannot even begin to list your names – family, friends, and strangers unaware – know that I love you. I could not have made it without you.

No portion of this book may be reproduced without the author's permission.

©Brilliant Star Press 2010

Healing from serious illness creates obligations to be more caring for the precious gift of life and to help others navigate the storm one has weathered.

Kenneth Cohen

Cohen, K. (2003). Honoring the Medicine: The Essential Guide to Native American Healing. New York, NY: Ballantine Books.

Introduction

I have often wondered how you summarize the events of your life in a few short pages, but then I realized a story is no different than a journey. The moments of my life unfold one step at a time and a record of those events appears on a page one word at a time. The task seems daunting, and over the years I have started and stopped never completing more than a page or two. My standstill was never the result of not feeling like I had something to say, but instead wondering if people would really be interested or care about my words.

My reluctance has often been fueled by my own personal fear and the projected fear of others. I hid my challenges at the advice of well meaning friends who feared for my career and felt that public admission would make me vulnerable to criticism. I have always feared rejection, and so have remained silent believing that if people really knew me they would not love me.

It is amazing the stories we tell ourselves! Few have any truth, but they sure are filled with a cast of characters and a whole lot of drama. Most of these stories are fueled by unconscious beliefs and are nothing more than fairy tales. We believe them to be true because through the year's life has become little more than a series of unconscious events. Instead of living I move through my day methodically, the moments lost in the monotony of my conditioned response. No thought is given to creating my life as I fall victim to the circumstances around me. Truth is whatever those perceived to be powerful say that it is and hectic schedules keep us from the silence that leads us to our own personal Truth.

It is time for me to speak. It is time for me to let go of my personal drama and let the cast of characters take their final bow. I am not my past and the baggage has to go! Unpacking has been sort of like opening Pandora's Box – a whole lot of ugly mingled with hope. The journey has been challenging and transforming. I looked death square in the eyes on several occasions and chose to live. I chose to be a victor and not a victim, powerful not powerless, and mindful not mindless.

Out Of Chaos Brilliant Stars Are Born is a collection of poems, personal reflection, and journal entries from my journey. In the moments of my life when it seemed like everything was coming unraveled, each of these threads was being woven into the loom of my tapestry. In those moments I was not privy to the big picture and was often blinded by the agony and pain. As the moments of my life continue to unfold my vision may be clearer and the path I travel less cluttered but by no means is my education complete. I will continue to grow, but I hope with a little more wisdom and a little less need for a wake up call.

Writing is my gift and the means through which I express some of my deepest emotions and thoughts. My intention in sharing my journey is to let my fellow sojourners know that they are not alone in what they feel or believe. I also hope to instill in all of you a hope that you can create a future full of love once you let go of the opinions of others and your own personal expectations and just -- Be.

So please sit down for a moment, away from the drama of life, quiet your mind, and enjoy.

Treasure yourself.

David J. Sterken

Personal Reflection: Growing Up

Childhood is a time of discovery and personal evolution. Beliefs about oneself are shaped as the result of relationships, circumstance, and culture. As an adult we must take responsibility for our choices, discover our own personal truth, and realize that we can/do co-create our experience either consciously or unconsciously.

As a child I always knew that I was *special,* but somewhere along the way that which I deemed *special*, other's labeled *different, strange,* and *sinful.* I did not understand my attraction to men, and I did not believe that it earned me the right to any less love than any other human being.

In Junior High I suddenly realized that to the world around me *gay* was a tem used in a very derogatory manner. I really did not understand what it meant to be gay, other than the fact that I knew I was attracted to men, nor did I know any other gay people. I struggled! I *knew* from somewhere deep inside me, that what I was being told was not Truth. Yet on some level, the constant bombardment of other's beliefs weakened by resolve, and I began to see myself as other's saw me.

My fear created a *way of living* shrouded by deception, an obsession to please, and overachievement. Over time these became the unconscious tools through which I experienced love in my life. Love became little more than an achievement. I *believed* that people cared more about *what I was (roles)* than *who I was (Truth).*

I suffered in silence, creating in my own mind assumptions and beliefs about people that only fueled the fire of my own fear. I never gave people the chance to love me for whom I was, because I wrongly believed that what I am is who I am.

Alone

This mask shields my true face
A charade that might make one think I am
Happy.
Yet if you would peel back this mask
You would find a soul that is...
Lonely and hurting.
One who yearns to hear the words, "I love you"

A Shell

Lord, I feel alone and as if no one really knows me.
I ache inside for someone to reach out and touch
    me
And simply say "I love you".
I hurt because it seems that no one really cares
    about the things I struggle with
And yet I fear that if people knew me I would
    suffer...
Rejection.
I long to throw off this exterior shell which is not
    really me
Yet it seems my only protection from the wagging
    tongues
Of those who really do not, nor wish to understand.
I want to cry but that would only rust my iron coat.
My only peace is that You love unconditionally
In that truth my weary soul rests.

Tears

It fell from my cheek unnoticed by many
From a soul that is weary, forlorn --
I long to be me, to peel off my mask
But to do so I feel would bring scorn.
So I live day by day in my tough outer shell
And to others appear happy, content
But once I'm alone the floodgates burst open
Wishing for someone to share my lament

Life is not a contest...

We live life as though it were some contest
Creating categories of – good, better, best
Always "trying" harder
Striving to become – become what?
More of this, less of that?

Isn't our journey really about
Fitting into our own skin –
Relaxing into the Creator
Discovering
The gifts and talents through which our actions
Speak the Language of Love

Life is NOT a contest
For there is no good, better, best
No gold, silver, and bronze medals
No success or failure

Life IS exploration, discovery
Learning, growth and...
Opportunity
To find the hidden aspects of ourselves
That yearns to be expressed,
The Voice of the soul – expressing through action
The Language of Love.

No gift or talent better or greater
Only vitality – life force
Translated through the one and only You.
Unique expression...
Yours – no contest,
Just an open channel
To – the Language of Love.

Santa Claus Thoughts

"I am imperfect and sinful by nature" – Santa Claus thought!

"Living the Christian life means that I will endure much hardship" – Santa Claus thought!

"Heaven is something that I experience at the end of my physical life" – Santa Claus thought!

"Humility means that I tolerate physical, emotional, and/or mental abuse" – Santa Claus thought!

"I must separate myself from those who believe and behave differently from me" – Santa Claus thought!

"God's children are only those who have asked Jesus to come into their heart" – Santa Claus thought!

Santa Claus thoughts – thoughts that are not true

Contracts and domesticated beliefs told and inflicted on us by

Forces outside of ourselves – people, society, social structures,

And those who make themselves the final authority on "truth".

Santa Claus thoughts – not – Ho, Ho, Ho

But – Oh, Oh, Oh!

Journal Entry (July 17, 1995)

Today, at 7:30 p.m., I learned I am HIV positive. I feel like I have been thrown headlong into a brick wall. I am numb. I cried, no sobbed, all through dinner. Do I have a future anymore? I was asked, "Do you know who infected you?" Does it matter? It won't change what has happened. Who do I tell?

Journal Entry (March 18, 2009)

I picked up one of my old journals today and read the thoughts I recorded soon after I was diagnosed with HIV. The denial was clearly evident and my words reminded screamed Pollyanna, and then suddenly -- silence. I had mastered covering up my feelings – "keeping a brave face" as some may call it. The pain was evident in the months, even years, of silence in my journal. I did write, but not for me, and not in my journal. Most of my writing was for the benefit of others, and while still soulful, between the accumulated layers of personal history my true story would unfold. I made choices driven by shame, guilt, and low self esteem that put me at risk for contracting HIV. My life was overshadowed by fear of rejection and abandonment, and as a young gay male I suffered significant depression. My identity was based on self-imposed labels and a belief system that while a good foundation, did not serve me. My search for identity, purpose, and meaning always drove me outside of myself to the voice of another. The answer is always in the silence – LISTEN!

Forgive Yourself...

Forgive yourself for becoming infected with HIV.
Your infection does not mean
That you are stupid, irresponsible,
Diminished.

The noise of life deafened you
To the whisper of your inner voice.
Without the guidance of your internal compass
You turned to external loci of control.
Limiting beliefs about yourself and the opinion of
    others
Created an illusion that love exists external to you.
Coupled with your personal history and desire for
    external validation
Your search for love took place at great personal
    risk.

I tried to call to you, but layers of hurt and
    disappointment
Created an impenetrable wall, my voice fell on deaf
    ears.
You journeyed further and further away from your
    destiny
Forgetting the Truth of who you are, the purpose
    of your incarnation.
I shouted -- hoping to awaken you from your
    slumber
Honoring the boundaries of free will – I waited.
I am essence – Love – I never change,
I cannot be diminished!

HIV is nothing more than shrill sound of an alarm
Stirring you from the slumber of an unconscious
    life.
As you wipe the sleep from your eyes,

Your vision penetrates the accumulated layers
Of emotional, psychological, mental, and spiritual
    reasoning
That shields you from The Truth.

I am noun and verb – I am Love – I am You.
Listen. Open your eyes. Live Truth.
Forgive yourself.

All I Wanted To Do Was Die

I remember a time when
All I wanted to do was die!
It was not a fleeting thought, for it lingered
Eleven years –
Not always conscious, but
Existing
On a deep subconscious level
Always.

I did not think I deserved to live
Because I believed what others said about me –
Unworthy, unclean, undesirable, unlovable!
My heart and my head try as they might
Could not shake those beliefs –
My actions self-destructive
Yet never "quite enough" to put me over the edge,
Although I teetered there many a time, because
All I wanted to do was die.

Belief led to shame
Feeding an already fragile mental state
And I remember a time when
All I wanted to do was die.

That time is now past.
Some fifteen months – of shifting consciousness
Changing belief, and
Listening to the voice of Truth.
Spirit's voice – a call from deep inside my Being,
Echoing through the sights and sounds of Nature,
The council of fellow sojourners, and
Wisdom literature.

I remember a time when
All I wanted to do was die, but
Now that time is past.
I long for the rising of the sun,
The opportunity that each new day brings –
Memory's fade giving rise to new belief, and
Truth declares itself in the quiet moments.
I listen – and in those moments declare

I want to live – not just today,
But for a thousand years

I Believe, Help My Unbelief

Spirit – I am whole,
My body, the house
Through which I express my internal
Perfection.
Yet some days this physical house succumbs to
Universal hypnotism – believing that what is
 happening in the
Physical world is truth.
I believe, help my unbelief!

Am I not a spiritual being having an earthly
 experience?
Yet my eyes sometimes see only ailment,
 woundedness
Illusions of a physical realm.
Dis-ease is little more than a call
From Spirit to recover
Balance of mind, body, and spirit.

Dear body – forgive me
For through my thoughts, actions, feelings, and
 beliefs
I have tilled the soil of
Condemnation.
Rather than nurturing the a spirit of wholeness and
 perfection
Which is my birthright.
I believe, help my unbelief

Barren

Barren – yes me, a male – barren
Not empty, for emptiness implies lack.
I feel barren!
Devoid of life and purpose,
The intercourse between my internal and external
　　　reality
Never impregnating to produce life --
Sterility fostered by an external perception of self
Job, other's opinions, labels –
Barren – devoid of all life and purpose.

Choices – miscarriage after miscarriage
Produce wounds and scars
Searching for self, love – always looking outside of
　　　me
Finding instead dis-ease – all hope fades
Life becomes little more than motions –
　　　unconscious existence.
Isolation only adds to my downward spiral
Barren – desiring only death
A glimpse in the mirror reveals only a shell
I stare – and in that moment – a quickening!

Three months, six months, now almost twelve
　　　months have past
The quickening, now an awakening of self
A consciousness borne of the eternal seed
Growing, kicking, moving, expanding
Barren – no longer
For now I am great with child!

Journal Entry (December 24, 2007)

Lessons from a snowflake...

As I gaze out the window snowflakes gently drift to the ground. I suddenly see the snowflake very differently and find even greater beauty in its presence and splendor. While I know that each one is unique, it is because they are unique that they possess extraordinary beauty. The snowflake's beauty lies beyond its perfection, for all snowflakes exist in a state of perfection. The beauty of the snowflake lies in the way that it expresses itself. Think for a moment what would happen if the snowflake decided to never fall from the sky. Who would see its beauty? It takes but one to tickle the nose of a child, a few more to build a snowman, but when joined in the beauty and perfection of others its gale force can shut down roadways, slow traffic, and bring life to a stand still.

Do you see yourself as a snowflake? Perfect, unique and beautiful in every way! There are no two alike. Just as there never has been, nor ever will be another YOU. So declare yourself! Does the snowflake worry when it is falling from the sky how it appears to the world? No – it does what the snowflake does – falls from the sky, glistening and beautiful. Reflecting the LIGHT where ever it is found. It doesn't worry about being beautiful because it just is beautiful.

As with the snowflake we are empowered when we acknowledge the beauty and gifts in our fellow man. What if we stopped expecting everyone to be "just like me" and encouraged them to declare themselves. The world would be taken by "storm"! Wars would end. Inequality would not exist. Diversity would prevail. And above everything else fear would be transformed into love. Think of the extraordinary beauty created by and snowfall. Do we dare to declare ourselves and let the beauty around us unfold?

Finally, perhaps one of the most miraculous things about a snowflake is its transformation. When it declares its extraordinary beauty to the world, and allows the snowflakes around it to express their perfection, it transforms -- nourishing the Earth with moisture. Even when we can no longer see or feel the snowflake's presence, it declares itself with the unfolding of the flowers in spring, the great oceans which teem with life, and the small brook whose music adds to the symphony of nature.

So you see the snowflake never dies – its form may change, but when it does what a snowflake is supposed to do its extraordinary power impacts not only the present moment, but life as it unfolds in the future.

Personal Reflection: Drug Addiction

As I gazed in the mirror I was horrified by my reflection. My addiction had reduced me to nothing more than a shell of a man. During the fall of 2006 I had dropped 30 pounds, my skin was gray, cheeks sunken, and eyes reflected back the emptiness I felt within. I had lost my spark; and life was nothing more than surviving until the next party. Isolation became my jailer as the shame and guilt associated with my addictive behavior led me further and further away from those who cared about me. The walls of my home were not a sanctuary, but the place that I would curl up in fetal position, drapes drawn, paranoid – alone.

On January 8, 2007 I teetered on the edge of life and death. I had been an addict for 11 years and slowly over time my passion for life began to ebb. Years of use had completely modified my brain chemistry. I never completely came down and my neurotransmitters were on such high alert that they never had an opportunity to fully recover. My body was always "on", a state of fight or flight, always demanding pleasure. Full recuperation rarely occurred and it was beginning to show. REM sleep never occurred and my nutritional state was very poor.

My addiction began in 1995 when I was diagnosed with HIV. The numbing effects of cocaine were transient and through the years I graduated to ecstasy, ketamine, crack, and finally settled on crystal meth (methamphetamine). Crystal meth is an interesting drug in that it can be consumed in a number of different ways. After snorting and smoking the drug I had finally settled on "slamming" (intravenous injection) because of the intensity and pleasure associated with the high.

My addiction was fed by the unhappiness in my life and false beliefs I held about myself. It would be correct to say that I was addicted to the way the drugs made me feel – powerful, fearless, attractive, and desirable. Crystal meth made me feel like I had just stepped into the phone booth and transformed into Superman, and stripped me of all inhibition. Imagine those feelings for an HIV+ man who on a regular basis experiences fatigue from his disease and treatment regime, feels ostracized by society and his own subculture, and feels "uncomfortable" in social situations. Being high was intoxicating! Psychological addiction fed into an already troubled self esteem and created a belief that I needed the drugs to unleash the real me that was inhibited by the walls I had built up over the years to protect me from the pain in my life.

Many people do not survive drug addiction and I know that I am fortunate to be alive. There were at least four times that due to my own carelessness I nearly overdosed, and as I stood looking at myself in the mirror in January 2008 I realized that this would be my defining moment. Who was this person staring back at me? The skin just hung on my bones. My muscled physique of which I had been so proud was now all but gone. I could barely walk as the crystal meth, due to my incessant use, was beginning to accumulate in my joints. My cheekbones had become very prominent due to weight loss and my eyes were sunken highlighted with dark circles. I looked like I should have been laid out in a casket. All life was gone. I felt nothing. As I gazed in the mirror I saw nothing but emptiness and pain. I must have stood there for at least ten minutes my eyes glazed over and then a miracle occurred.

A single tear fell on my cheek. I remember being jarred out of my trance like state. It had been months since I had experienced any type of emotion except paranoia. Life had become little more than existence. Another tear fell and soon water was cascading down my cheeks. At that moment I saw clearly for the first time in my life! No walls, no haze, no layers, no shadows – only light – shining from the very core of my being. A glimpse ever so briefly of true essence – spirit – beyond label, perception, belief – Divine.

You cannot walk away from an experience like that unchanged? I have no need to try and explain the events of that day. Miracles happen all the time, but in the busyness of our lives they often go unnoticed. What I do know is that I walked away from that experience totally transformed. The fire and passion in my life no longer comes from a man made synthetic substance igniting the pleasure centers in my brain, but from an internal flame fueled by a desire to live purposefully and love passionately.

It's Just Recreational

I can stop using crystal meth anytime, after all
It's just recreational.

I usually pick some up on Friday night to get my
    weekend started.
It's just recreational.

I usually go out with friends on Saturday night,
But since I didn't sleep at all on Friday night
I buy two more quarter baggies.
It's just recreational.

I go to an after bar party Saturday night
A dealer at the party has "some really good stuff"
I buy a couple more quarter bags for next weekend
It's just recreational.

I get home at 7:00 a.m. – I am dragging a little bit
I take a couple bumps to get me through Sunday
    brunch.
It's just recreational.

I crawl into bed on Sunday at 9:00 p.m.
I don't sleep very well – tossing and turning
Jarred awake by body twitches,
REM sleep never comes – because of use.
It's just recreational.

Monday morning I am dragging
Coffee does little to energize me
"I'll just do a bump to get me going."
It's just recreational.

By Thursday the weekends sleep deprivation
Has got the best of me,
I feel depressed, as the neurotransmitters in my brain
Attempt to reestablish chemical balance.
I'm dragging physically
"Perhaps a couple little bumps won't hurt,
After all tomorrow's Friday and I have the weekend to recover."
I do a line.
It's just recreational.

Soon I "need" it to get through my day.
The weekends start on Thursday and spill over to Tuesday.
I never actually come down, but
It's just recreational.

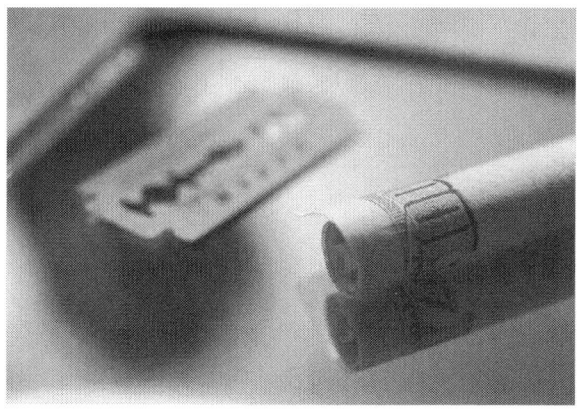

Fix

Desperate – phone calls
Looking for a score
Using next weeks grocery money
Rent
Cash advance on credit cards
Fix

Desperate – scrapping baggies
Hoping for enough residual
For a hit
Fix

Desperate – sweating
Coming down
NO, NO, NO not yet!
Phone rings
Score – Yes!
Fix

Desperate – pacing
Doorbell, delivery
Ten dollars short
"Front me until tomorrow?"
I gotta have my
Fix

Desperate – preparation
Elastic strap
Veins are tired
Nothing pops out
Dehydrated
Fix

Desperate – I poke
And poke
Veins blow, bruised
Frustrated – I need my
Fix

Desperate – no success
After 90 minutes
My arms look like a pin cushion
I will have to wear long sleeves
I lay down
Sleep

On my bedside table
The syringe waits
Beckoning
Fix!

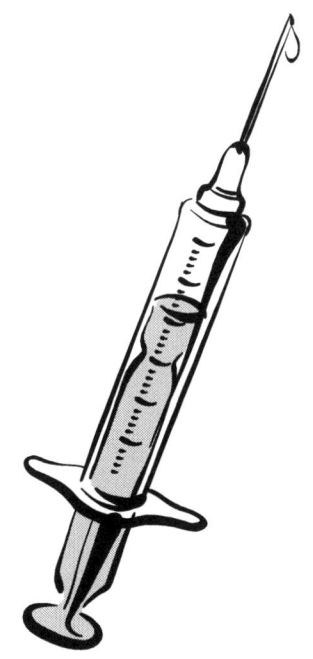

Hit

I crush the crystals into powder
And watch as it dissolves.
No remnants of its original form
Just a clear liquid
By all appearances – harmless.

How much is too much —
A quarter or a half?
Will it create enough edge –
Or stop my heart?
Should I play it safe – or go for
Just a little more than last time?
Better to play it safe – I remember
Too much – panicked, unable to walk,
Heart palpitations, nearly passing out –
Thinking death was imminent.

The tourniquet forces my veins to plump up
An easy target as the needle breaks the skin.
Flash – blood fills the syringe
A gentle tug release the tourniquet
Gentle pressure on the plunger of the syringe
Sends this synthetic man made chemical
Into my sterile blood stream.

I cough. My heart flutters.
I am forced to take a deep breath.
A sudden surge of pleasure, and
All inhibition is gone.
I am the center of the Universe
It is all about me.

I seek physical pleasure,
Taking great risk.
The cost to me long term is great
Physically, mentally, emotionally, and spiritually
But in those moments I give little thought
To the long term consequence of
The hit.

Fire In My Vein

The needle, the flash of blood
Inject –
Feelings of ecstasy, power
Inhibition completely dissolves.
I am at the mercy of a synthetic compound
Over stimulated pleasure centers
Flooded with dopamine.
I am hyper alert, energetic, fearless
Addicted to the "feeling"
But numb to the devastation
Mentally, physically, emotionally and spiritually.

The need for the "feeling" fuels my addiction
Yet the fire in my vein
Reeks havoc on my body –
Gray skin, sunken cheeks, darting eyes
Weight loss of thirty pounds –
Little more than a shell – "existing"
Empty – searching – lonely
Isolation, shame.
The fire in my vein – creating the illusion
Of power and confidence – yet
All the while creating a dependence
On a "feeling" – artificially induced
By the fire in my vein.

The shadows ever so subtly obscuring the Light
Creeping closer to the edge – the precipice – I
    teeter
Life and death – the fire in my vein demands more!
I gaze into the mirror and see only remnants
Of what I used to be – a shell
A tear lands on my cheek – HOPE!

The fire in my vein demands more –
Another tear falls – LIGHT!
I drop the syringe –
I see like I have never seen before
Beyond "physical" – my spiritual essence –
LIGHT – flickering – waiting only to be fanned,
Igniting purpose and passion, creating LIFE,
Immersed in LOVE.

I have never again picked up a syringe
I have no need of the fire in my vein
For a fire has ignited in my soul
Fueled by the desire to live purposefully...
And love passionately!

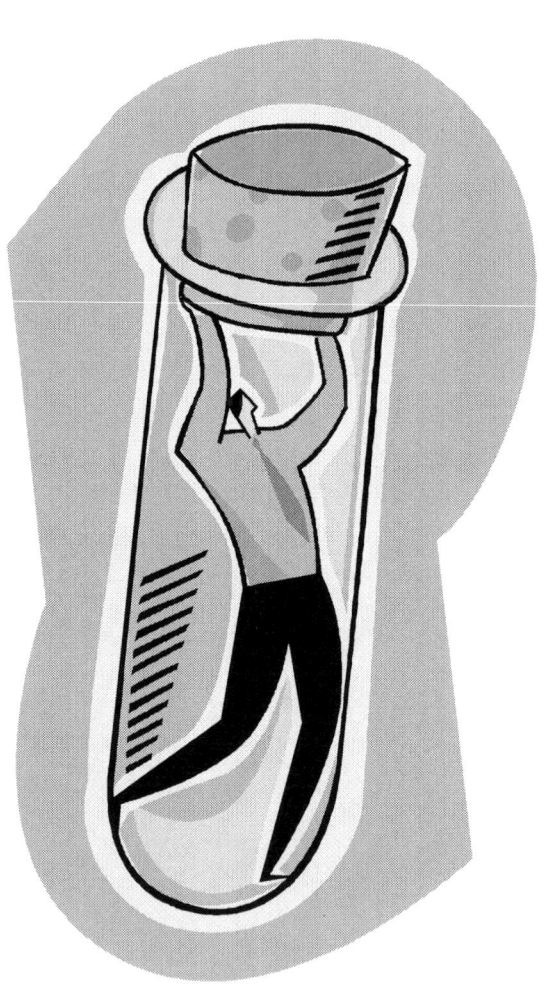

Getting Unstuck...

I wake up most mornings thinking about the day
Not with excitement and enthusiasm --
But feeling stuck!

There is no spring in my step, no drive to –
Get up and go to work.
I feel stuck – trapped!
Weighed down – "doing" – simply "because"
No fire or passion.
Sighs – often, heaviness bearing down upon my
Spirit – I feel stuck!

I don't want to be stuck anymore –
How do I proceed?
No one can do it for me. Go within –
Find your passion and purpose,
Reconnect!
Don't settle for – "just because"
Take charge, create your day consciously.
Say no! Remember it is not about "just because",
Or – because no one else will do it.

Getting unstuck is "doing" because I want to –
Doing – aligns with MY purpose and passion
It creates that little wiggle
Or shift – that MUST happen for me to
Get unstuck!

Cocoon

I've lived within the walls of a cocoon.
Enveloped in the darkness of limited ideas
About myself and my abilities --
My quarters were tight with little room to wiggle
Sometimes the darkness seemed thrust upon me
By forces external
Outside – seemingly powerful, learned, elder –
Living "truth" literally, historically – final
With no room for emerging thought
In a dynamic environment of change.

I lived within the walls of a cocoon
Enveloped in the darkness of limited ideas,
But Light cannot be extinguished by the darkness
Enveloped perhaps – but NEVER extinguished!
A spark need only ignite and soon
Glowing embers become a flame
The realization of TRUE SELF.

In that moment the walls of the cocoon
Seemed little more than fragile paper
And as the Light penetrated every cell,
Every molecule – even DNA
I was transformed – by the renewing of my mind!
I emerged from prison with wings
Taking flight for the first time in my life –
Understanding at last what it means to be truly
FREE.

Process...

I looked through my scrapbook today
So many snapshots – memories
Of a single moment in time
Snapshots – illusions
Focus on what is now
But never capture
Process.

Process – atoms dancing all around us
Connecting with each other.
Interbeing – the bigger Reality
To which we are all connected.
There is great change occurring all the time
Around us, within us
Trust it
Surrender to it
Process.

Process – often beyond our control
To fight it is like trying to swim –
Upstream.
Relax into the Process
It is vastly loving.
Let it carry you down the stream of Life
Process.

I looked through my scrapbook today
So many snapshots
They are not Me
For I am ever becoming
Changing – with the dawn of each new day
Process.

Proverbs 3:5-6

*Trust in the Lord with all your heart
And lean not unto your own understanding
In all your ways acknowledge Him
And He will direct your paths.*

Trust – the collision of Divine Nature and Human Heart
Perfection and perception,
Connecting at the level of feeling
Not just partially, completely.
A synergism so amazing, miraculous
That it draws you into "moment" – not future or past,
Defying explanation or understanding.

Trust – acknowledges the Humanity of experience
But draws us inward, away from the drama
Of our perceived reality, toward a Divine solution.

Trust beckons us to loosen our grip on
Attachments and limiting beliefs
By acknowledging our own tunnel vision.
Getting out of our own head – ideas
And surrendering to Divine Mind –
A "bigger picture", often obscured
By the emotion of our Humanity and personal myopia.

Trust is about flexibility and flow,
Not being tied to a particular outcome,
Releasing control, and the need to be right.
Surrendering "all", not just the convenient, and
Relaxing into the groundlessness of circumstance.

Fear moves us closer to Truth
Our desire for escape, closer to Divine
Letting go we awaken
Allowing room for ALL that is to happen.
We feel with every ounce of our Humanity, and
TRUST.

Personal Reflection: Awakening "Worth"

Self-worth and self-esteem are two terms that are often used interchangeably – in fact Webster defines self-worth as self-esteem. I would propose to you however, that the terms in reality reflect radically different ideas.

Let us begin by removing "self" from each of the terms. *Esteem* is defined as a *"judgment" or "opinion"* – in short it is how we feel about ourselves. Esteem can be rocked by circumstance and unconsciously shaped by the opinion of another. Conceptually, it is fluid in evolution, formed by outside motivators and internal monitors. Since "esteem" is nothing more than "opinion" it cannot be substantiated by direct proof or knowledge. In simple terms it is little more than an estimate of one's value or worth.

Worth, by definition, is a quality – which distinguishes it as *a part of an individual's makeup*. Since it is a part of our biology it is permanent, and cannot be diminished by person(s) or circumstance. Worth – begins in the mind of God, is manifest at conception, and miraculously demonstrated through the unique journey of each individual. Worth cannot be taken away from you for it is part of your inherent nature. You are created worthy!

Despite the fact that each of us was born worthy, awakening *worth* is a journey of self-discovery. Many of us approach life and relationships from a philosophy of lack – believing that joining with another or success (e.g. money, job, recognition) will fill the void and make us complete. Yet it is an oxymoron to attempt to become "more complete" when you are complete already.

Our worth is not defined by physical appearance, ability or skill – but instead in the purposeful journey of self-discovery through utilization of our unique gifts and abilities. So many of us spend our lives trying to *do* better, perhaps instead of spending so much of our time *doing* we should focus our attention on just *being*.

Many religions teach that man was born lacking and must strive to become more complete. This continued striving toward perfection widens the gap between God and man and creates separation rather than oneness. Being created in the "image of God" implies a close or exact resemblance – how will our striving improve that image?

I will say it once again – stop spending so much time *doing* and instead focus on *being*. The bumps in our personal journey are because we get in our own way. Stop trying to prove yourself – you are worthy! Stop trying to be perfect – instead strive to be whole. Self-esteem can very quickly be influenced by public opinion, failure, and less than optimal circumstance. Self-worth is the cornerstone of life upon which, through the discovery and utilization of our gifts, we find purpose.

It has taken me 40 years to discover that no one can give you worth. My words or actions might increase my self esteem, but worth is something that can be neither given nor taken away by mere mortal man. Our existence is more than our physical essence – which fades with time. Our worth begins in the intangible realm of spirit, and only through *knowing* and *being* does it take on a physical form.

If Life Is An Occasion...

If life is an occasion, should I not awaken everyday with
Anticipation and excitement –
Realizing I have a clean slate on which to create this
Masterpiece I call – life.

If life is an occasion, should not my thoughts be filled with
Possibility and extraordinary wonder
As I look all around me and see
Miracles unfolding.

If life is an occasion, should I not dress up
Like I would for any special event –
And clothe myself in a Spirit of
Love, gratitude, humility and compassion.

If life is an occasion, should not my toes tap,
And my feet dance to the sounds of nature –
The symphony swells within my Spirit, and
I feel connected to every living thing.

If life is an occasion, should I not surround myself
With people that support me through
Word and action, for in so doing
I attract only that which is good to my life.

If life is an occasion, every minute is filled with
Opportunity – new people, new experiences
Beckoning each of us to – rise to it!

If life is an occasion

The Eyes of Elizabeth (Luke 1:39-45)

The eyes of Elizabeth – we know not their hue
They may have been brown, or they could have
    been blue.
Farsighted, nearsighted – we never will know
But was it "eyesight" or "insight" her lesson
    bestows.

History, and "packaging" – all outer shell
Attachment, perception, did not story tell.
Instead in her greeting to Mary her kin
She opened her heart to see Christ within.

The past did not matter, the future a risk?
She saw only "essence" which always persists!
And there in that moment her heart burst into song
Connection – the thing for which each one of us
    long.

Connection by blood – yes, but oh so much more,
Namaste'—recognition of the very essence she
    bore.

The eyes of Elizabeth we know not their hue
They may have been brown, or they may have
    been blue
The lesson they teach us dear sister and brother
Is to see and nurture the Christ in each other.

Inspired by Reverend Marty Rienstra's sermon – The Risk of Christmas (December 16, 2007)

Personal Reflection: Deskunking

My friends,

This week has been an extraordinary week of insight and learning. The lessons were not offered through the "words" of scholars or pages of a textbook -- but through he eyes of creatures with four legs and fur and beaks and feathers. Native Americans teach us that "humanity is part of nature, and nature is a part of itself" (Andrews, 2005) -- in essence the Hermetic Law of Correspondence -- that all things are connected and have significance.

As many of you know last year I adopted 2 dogs from the animal shelter. Maxwell -- my chocolate poodle -- is one of those creatures that just loves life and any and all creatures -- no matter how big or small. He has absolutely no fear and approaches life from a friendly and loving perspective. This week his loving spirit got him in a little trouble when he tried to make friends with a skunk. He meant the skunk no harm he just wanted to play -- but the skunk didn't know that and mounted his best defense. Pew! How often do we withdraw in fear from opportunities to make new friends? The events of our life often create "walls" -- perceived or real -- that prevent us from taking that first step to reach out and offer a friendly or loving gesture. Maxwell only sees a playmate or friend when he encounters people or animals -- he cares very little about how they look, smell, or what they have to offer him. He is only concerned about the moment and what fun may occur as a result of the experience. He does not let his past experience color his present moment --

as I am quite certain he would walk right back up to the skunk and offer his friendship once again.

The skunk offers incredible symbolic meaning if you can get past the smell. Although the "spray does not kill, it awakens a healthy respect in those who encounter it" (Andrews 2005). The skunk is self-assured and confident in itself -- it does not get out of the way of any other animal. When a skunk shows up as a totem "you are going to have opportunities to bring out new respect and self-esteem. People are going to notice you. How they notice you and remember you can be controlled by you" (Andrews, 2005). Unfortunately the skunk is most often remembered for its odor. But if you have ever had to the opportunity to watch one from a distance it is a beautiful creature -- yet in order to "protect itself" it throws up its tail in defense. It is unlikely that it will ever have friends because all it ever sees is threat. Fear has so captivated its life that the skunk always has to keep others at arms length. Do you see the tremendous symbolism behind this animal? Every encounter I have with another will leave a residual mark -- it can either be an encounter growing out of a spirit of love and kindness or does the stench of the past prevent you from extending yourself.

In the midst of all the deskunking and listening to the lessons offered through the whispers of nature I experienced yet another unusual encounter while letting the dogs frolic in the freshly fallen snow. As we played in the backyard overhead a flock of perhaps 50 crows landed in the tress surrounding my yard and proceeded to call to each other. The sound was incredible -- so much so that it caused my puppies to stop, look up in the air and cock there heads as if to say -- "what is all the racket about?" Native American's believe the call of the crow is a reminder that "magic and creation are potentials very much alive every day" (Andrews, 2005). We need only look for the opportunities to manifest the magic of life -- it is available to us everyday. It is also a reminder that we can create a vibrant life filled with opportunity.

Three separate lessons but in my opinion all lead up to one meaning -- when we manifest love in our lives everyday is filled with magic and opportunity. The fear of another should not dissuade us from what our heart knows that it should do -- even if our first encounter is met with obvious resistance. Often the resistance in another is simply a result of their past, and in some it is so ingrained that they just naturally react. The true test for us is when we can look beyond the natural defenses of another and see the true spirit of the individual. This is magic and when you act from love rather than fear opportunities emerge.

Namaste my friends.

Reference: Andrews, T. (2005). Animal Speak: The Spiritual and Magical Powers of Creatures Great and Small. St. Paul, MN: Llewellyn Publications

Today I Untied My Shoes..

We spend so much of our lives running --
Away from that which was, and
Toward that which might never be?
Fear, perception, unhealthy self regard, and
  external "noise"
Fuel the steps of our marathon.
A treadmill of disappointment, and
A list of things that always seem just beyond our grasp.

Today I untied my shoes and took them off.

A snowflake gently landed on my cheek. It was
  cold.
A train whistle sounded in the distance, warning of its approach.
A raccoon slid across the ice in the neighbor's yard.
I laughed.
This is being present – this is moment.

Today I untied my shoes and took them off.
I listened. I took a breath. I saw.

Today I untied my shoes and took them off.
Today I began my journey.
I choose to walk – barefoot.

Release…

I picked up my journal.
The pages filled with memories of
Pain.
My body remembers –
Triggering my unconscious psyche.
Awash with conflicting emotion
I succumb to ego
Feeling fragile and defeated –
Release.

Fear binds me to the wounds of my past.
I suffer in isolation.
Ideas about me, and how I "think" people will react
Only tend to imprison my mind
Tightening the grip of ego upon me
Release.

Limiting beliefs cloud my personal vision –
I have forgotten who I am –
Love – my essence!
Wholeness and Perfection – my state!

I stand on my growing edge.
I claim my destiny.
I consciously choose release.
I release!

Twinkles...

Twinkles – what are they?
A tradition handed down from the High Priestess of
　　Play
To celebrate an opening of oneself
Recognition for discovery
Deep work.

Not thunderous applause – loud.
Twinkles – gentle accolades
Honoring, acknowledging... as one releases
Fear, attachment, and limiting beliefs.
Transformation.

Twinkles – gentle reminders
That while life may at times take on a serious tone
The "spirit" with which you approach your deep
　　work
May remain lighthearted and playful.
Connection with your inner child.

Twinkles – the gentle fluttering of fingers
Positive energy – directed, shimmering, powerful
Creating a smile.
Twinkles!

In honor of David Gershon and Gail Straub (The High Priestess of Play)

White Knuckles…

I hold onto you so tightly my knuckles are white.
My fingers cramp, it has been 14 years and I have
    not let go.
You color every moment of my existence – my
    relationships,
Sense of self, even my career – it is though I see
    the world
Through HIV colored glasses – limitation,
    woundedness.
I often cry – not just tears, but from the depth of
    my Being
Trying to understand – I hold onto you so tightly
    my knuckles are white.
"I will not let you go until you bless me!"

I wrestle with the shadows of my past, the
    unconscious choices
That brought me to this place – karma,
    consequence.
Repeated patterns of behavior – fear.
They no longer work for me, I feel restless,
    desperate, frightened
I cry out – I loosen my grip – my knuckles are pink.

HIV – you do not define me, I am not a label
Male, gay, nurse, brother, uncle – these are just
    the wrapping
The outer expression – the house, temple
In which resides the Truth of my Being
A unique vibration of Love, bestowed with
    extraordinary gifts
Unlike any other – Perfection.
My fingers relax – the color returns to my skin.

A limiting belief fueled the unconscious behavior
    that led me to this place
The notion that Love is "achieved", "found",
    "sought after"
A marathon of effort, when in Truth it is our
    Essence
Always present, of endless supply – Existence.

Truth cripples the false self – it no longer has a
    "hold" on me
This is my blessing – I let go
Transformation!

In The Morning...

The sky is illuminated with color
Brilliant pink, orange, and blue –
As the sun rises to proclaim the dawning
Of a new day – opportunity.

I stir – the sunbeams beckon me to awaken
My first thought is of you.
I smile.
My heart beat quickens
Your love washes over me
Penetrating every cell in my body
I feel safe – loved.

The boys and I wander outside
The birds welcome our rising
Singing the song of love
Declaring its presence throughout all of creation.
I listen – my eyes glisten with tears
Consciously I throw my head back in laughter
And silently mouth these words to the Universe
"Thank you, thank you, thank you."

In the morning –
I acknowledge my gift.
It is a conscious effort, born out of years of
    searching.

In the morning –
I renew my love for you
Out of the desire to maximize the moments
And minimize the minutia.

In the morning –
I seize the opportunity to nurture our relationship
Creating an environment that foster our growth
Individually and as a couple.

In the morning.

I love you today...

I love you today -- means I recognize that you are emerging and growing every day as you discover your talents and purpose.

I love you today -- means I accept you for who you are in this moment of time.

I love you today -- means that how I feel about you is not minimized by circumstance or action.

I love you today -- means I always respect your opinion, knowing that it does not have to be my own.

I love you today -- means I am not threatened by others you call "friend", for life is filled with teachers and fellow sojourners.

I love you today -- means that I can express how MY heart feels, without expecting/needing you to feel the same way about me.

I love you today -- means I cherish every single minute that we have together -- however, we choose to spend it!

I love you today -- means that I consciously acknowledge daily the privilege that has been extended to me, by you, to share your life. This privilege I neither take lightly nor allow myself to become too comfortable that I take you for granted.

I love you today -- means that I own my feelings, share then with you in openness and honesty, and never wield them as a tool of harm or manipulation.

I love you today -- means that with you I seek to create a condition of optimal well-being, which allows us to grow physically, mentally, emotionally, socially, and spiritually.

I love you today -- means that I attempt to empower you to love and nurture yourself in order to foster a state of being that is encompassed by balance, peace of mind, contentment, high self-esteem, self-acceptance, and intimacy.

I love you today -- means just this -- I love you today -- and with the dawn of each new day -- once again I have the wonderful opportunity to "love you today".

My Little Adonis…

My Adonis – my Greek god – with golden locks and
    eyes of blue
What was it that drew my heart to you?
Our universes have existed as parallel paths
Never coming together, and then
As if your soul called to me
I suddenly heard your voice
My heart leapt
We connected
And I knew that my search was over.

I have been looking for you
All of my life.
I knew you were out there –
I could feel your presence,
The journey has been long and hard
But necessary – preparation
Molding me and making me into who I am
Today.

I love myself – and because I do -- I can love you
Mind, body, and soul.
My heart is a well spring of emotions and feelings
That I cannot explain…
And feel no necessity to do so.
You understand – and feel it too
Connection – love
Beyond our mind's comprehension.
More than a feeling of butterflies in our stomach
True, authentic
A beginning that is new with the rising of the sun.
A fire that remains at the end of the day.
I love you.

I will proclaim my love for you by shouting it from
 the mountaintops
So that all may hear, and,
Then whisper those same words
Gently in your ear –
My little Adonis – I love you –
Now and forever – with every breath that I
 breathe.

Take flight with me now as we begin our life
together.

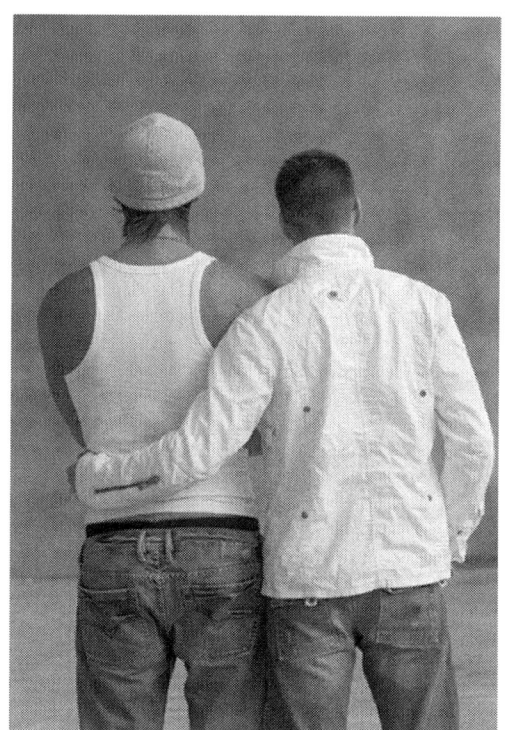

Personal Reflection: Loving Another

Loving someone means that sometimes you have to get out of the way so they can learn. A child learns to successfully walk, not when a parent hovers over them, but when a parent stands aside and lets them fall, get back up, and take a few more steps.

I am learning that loving someone sometimes means watching them from a distance as they journey toward whatever destination life has for them. It is also the realization that although I would like to save others from the pain and hurt I went through; some must experience it for themselves. My job is to get out of the way and allow Spirit to work. Be large enough to back off and allow another to test their wings.

I Held Your Hand...

I held your hand. The veins bulged – blue – against the pallor of your skin. That skin – it seems nothing more than a thin veil on your five foot two, sixty pound frame. Disease has taken its toll, leaving your body a mere skeleton. I held your hand.

I held your hand. In that sacred moment I recognized that we only had moments, while I still wished for time. I told you that I loved you and that I would be fine, although secretly I could not imagine my life without you. We had spent so much time laughing, and now I could feel a void opening in the very depths of my soul   I held your hand.

I held your hand. As you whispered, "I love you" a deep well opened inside me, sending glistening droplets of water cascading down my cheeks. I held your hand – more tightly.

I held your hand. In that same moment you uttered the words that I feared the most, yet anticipated with a heavy heart. "I am tired, and it's time for me to go." How could I let you go? I held your hand.

I held your hand. I watched you close your eyes. I gently kissed you. I sat with you for a few more moments, not wanting to let go, but knowing that it was time to let another – hold your hand.

In loving memory of my mother – Dorothy Belle Sterken

It's Time For Me To Shine...

I have resisted life – believing a disease
Could diminish me and limit my possibility.
I had an idea – that drugs could take away pain
And create feelings of power and invulnerability.
My resistance left me raw, numb, and empty.

The chaos in my life was of my own doing
Afraid of "me" – my power, my possibility.
Attempts to fan my internal flame
Never successful – mere sparks
Extinguished as I wrestled against ideas and beliefs
    about myself
Trying hard to paddle upstream
Clinging to the rocks and dead trees --
Debris scattered throughout "the river" – my
    journey.

It's time for me to shine.
To acknowledge my own brilliance
My possibility.
To stop fighting, the movement of life
And allow the current to turn me
In the direction of my natural inheritance.

It is time for me to shine,
To follow my bliss,
To listen to my gut,
And become.

It is time for me to shine!

"I Sight"

The alarm jars me awake
I open my eyes allowing them to adjust
To the streams of light pouring through the window shades,
It is a new day – opportunity, possibility
A clean slate – pristine, unchartered
My "I sight" – 20/20.

And then it starts – life!
My "I sight" quickly veiled by circumstance
Blurred by the baggage of my life – personal history
Vision now becomes a reflection of
Opinion, belief, thought, fear.
Now farsighted – my "I sight" is obscured
I quickly forget – clean slate – pristine, unchartered.
I settle in to comfortable, convenient, unconscious–
The day has no passion, vision
I go through the motions – squinting, unable to focus
My "I sight" is fuzzy – 20/80.

At the end of the day I am fatigued
So much of my time has been spent "performing"
Perceived expectations – created in my own mind
Not often verified, clarified -- lies
A false lens through which I see
Self – personal history, baggage
I close my eyes in sleep
My "I sight" damaged – 20/200

The alarm jars me awake
It is a new day – opportunity, possibility
A clean slate – pristine, unchartered
A corrective lens
My "I sight" – 20/20

Life…

Life – what is it?
An alarm clock jars us from a peaceful sleep
Sending us on our way to jobs or events – where
    we –
Simply watch the clock as it announces
The end of another day.
We are propelled into
Traffic, events, obligations.
Finally home, the remote activates
"The tube".   We land on the couch
Hypnotized – mindless.
Bedtime – and within a matter of hours
The cycle repeats itself!
Is this life?

Life – five hundred twenty five thousand six
    hundred minutes --
In a year -- multiplied by seventy years
That's like a gazillion – opportunities.
Every second offers – mindfulness.
Sight, texture, sound, color, flavor, variety –
    opportunity to
Laugh until you cry, splash in puddles, love,
Smell a daffodil, feel the sand between your toes,
Make new friends, watch the sunsets,
Listen to the wind – this is life!

Life is an occasion – rise to it!

My New Name...

Experience and circumstance have changed me
Transformation – thought and belief evolve
The walls of past crumble, seeming protection –
But in truth, barriers which have obscured my True
    Self.

My new name – Brilliant Star – borne out of my
    desire
To shed the beliefs of a social reality, the opinion of
    others
That I accepted as Truth -- their fear
Which became mine, creating farsightedness –
Blurring my vision to that which was right in front
    of me –
True Self.

Despite the shadows of my past, the seeming
    chaos
That seemed to follow me; my Light could not be
    extinguished!
Smoldering embers waiting for the breath of Spirit
To reignite the flame of Divine – soul
    consciousness –
Memory of my distinct purpose, a "knowing" so
    deep
That my DNA quivers creating a natural luminosity
Visible as my dreams unfold, glorious, magnificent,
Clear and full of Light – Brilliant!

I twinkle in recollection of my celestial body
As my inner God-spark, radiates outward,
Sending Light in all directions –
Metamorphosis of thought and belief
Create new action, reaction to circumstance

I have a new name, birthed out of the chaos of my life —
I am Brilliant Star!

A portion of the proceeds from the sale of this book will benefit

the grand rapids Red project
improving health : preventing HIV : reducing risk

Visit their website at *www.redproject.org*

You may contact David via email at
tattoos4016@comcast.net

Made in the USA
Charleston, SC
16 February 2010